FRANCE

ABDO
Publishing Company

FRANCE

by Ida Walker

Content Consultant
Stephen A. Schuker
Professor, University of Virginia, Department of History

CREDITS

Published by ABDO Publishing Company, 8000 West 78th Street, Edina, Minnesota 55439. Copyright © 2012 by Abdo Consulting Group, Inc. International copyrights reserved in all countries. No part of this book may be reproduced in any form without written permission from the publisher. The Essential Library™ is a trademark and logo of ABDO Publishing Company.

Printed in the United States of America,
North Mankato, Minnesota
062011
092011

 THIS BOOK CONTAINS AT LEAST 10% RECYCLED MATERIALS.

Editor: Erika Wittekind
Copy Editor: Susan M. Freese
Series design and cover production: Emily Love
Interior production: Kazuko Collins

About the Author: A native of Iowa, Ida Walker earned a degree with honors in museum studies from the University of Northern Iowa. She did graduate work in art history and museum studies at Syracuse University. She is a freelance editor and author living in upstate New York.

Library of Congress Cataloging-in-Publication Data
Walker, Ida.
 France / by Ida Walker.
    p. cm.
 Includes bibliographical references and index.
 ISBN 978-1-61783-109-6
 1. France--Juvenile literature. I. Title.
 DC17.W35 2011
 944--dc23
                                        2011019249

Cover: The Louvre Museum in Paris, France

TABLE OF CONTENTS

CHAPTER 1
A VISIT TO FRANCE

A crackle comes over the speaker, and then you hear, "*Bienvenue à Paris!*
This is your pilot, and on behalf of the entire flight crew, welcome to
Paris!" Having completed a seven-hour flight from New York City, you are
ready to deplane and begin your visit to France.

As you walk through Terminal 1 at Charles de Gaulle International
Airport, you notice how busy it is. There are food courts, duty-free shops,
and Internet kiosks almost everywhere you look. You soon find the spot
to catch the Réseau Express Régional (RER), the commuter train to Paris,
and hop onboard for the 14-mile (23-km) trip.

EXPLORING PARIS

The view from your hotel room is almost too much to take in. You can
see part of the Eiffel Tower, even though your hotel isn't exactly in the
center of Paris. You grab your guidebook and start to think about all of

**One of the best views of Paris, also known as the City of Light,
is from the top of the Eiffel Tower.**

EIFFEL TOWER

The Eiffel Tower was designed as the entrance to the Universal Exposition of 1889, a world's fair to commemorate the 100-year anniversary of the French Revolution. Although today the Eiffel Tower is considered an architectural and engineering marvel, many architectural critics hated it when it first opened. Some called to have it torn down, and it was supposed to be demolished after 20 years. By then, however, it had become a popular attraction and a valuable communications tool for radio antennae, so it was spared. During the early battles of World War I, the French Army used the tower to dispatch taxis carrying men to the front.

the places you want to visit. Of course, you will tour the famous art museum, the Louvre, as well as the Arc de Triomphe, which honors the individuals who fought and died for France during the French Revolution and Napoleonic Wars. You also want to visit the Cathédrale Notre-Dame de Paris, one of the most famous churches in the world, and, just outside Paris, the Palace of Versailles, which served as a royal residence and the site of many treaties. But all these sights will wait until tomorrow or the next day. Right now, you want to explore.

As you step onto the sidewalk, one word comes to mind: crowded. There are people as far as you can see. You blend into the crowd and are soon part of the jostling mass of humanity.

Quickly, you discover the variety of shops on the streets of Paris. The appetizing smells of freshly baked bread and freshly brewed coffee draw you into one of the many bakeries, cafés, and coffee shops. Curiosity

Built for the Universal Exposition of 1889, the Eiffel Tower serves
as a communications tower.

THE CITY OF LIGHT

One of Paris's best-known nicknames is the "City of Light," or *la Ville Lumière*.[1] Although the nickname itself is well known, how it originated is unclear. Some people believe it dates back to the city's role as the center of global culture during the eighteenth century's Age of Enlightenment. Another theory traces the nickname back to the early use of gas streetlights on the Champs-Élysées, a main Parisian thoroughfare.

lures you through the door of a butcher shop, where meats of all kinds hang from hooks and fill display cases. Next, you find a shop devoted to cheese—more kinds than you could ever imagine. Then, out of the corner of your eye, you see a familiar site: McDonald's. Since you are in Paris, you pass on by, deciding to forgo the familiar in favor of the new.

The shops lining the streets of Paris offer more than food and drink, however. There are bookstores, jewelry stores, and fashion boutiques. Street musicians provide entertainment for shoppers and passersby.

As you make your way through Paris, you also discover another characteristic of this city: heavy traffic. Trying to cross the street sometimes borders on being dangerous, as the blare of a car horn warns you that the driver may not yield the right of way. Nevertheless, dodging traffic seems to add another thrill to this already exciting city.

The Arc de Triomphe, one of the best-known monuments of Paris, was completed in 1836.

After spending hours discovering some of Paris's many shops and cafés, you decide to end your first day with a walk along the Seine River. The crowd has thinned, and you feel a sense of calm. As you take a quiet stroll along the banks of the Seine, you catch a familiar sight: a small Statue of Liberty, similar to the one that stands in New York Harbor. The original, a gift to the United States from France in 1886, certainly remains the most famous, but other versions of Lady Liberty exist, including the one that stands in front of you. You finish your walk and return to your hotel to contemplate the rest of your trip.

RECOVERING FROM WAR

Paris received relatively slight damage during the world wars. But elsewhere in France, the sites where shops, homes, and other buildings now stand were once filled with rubble. Both World War I (1914–1918) and World War II (1939–1945) were devastating to the country. As the German Luftwaffe and other air forces bombed French cities, citizens scurried to take shelter and dodged debris falling from buildings that had been struck. Besides the physical destruction of the country, many people were killed. The loss of life was particularly high during World War I.

Throughout France, numerous sites honor war heroes, especially those who gave their lives to free France from German control. Visitors can travel to the coast to Normandy, the site of the D-day invasion on June 6, 1944. There, they can pay their respects to the servicemen who stormed the beach, most of whom were Americans and Britons.

A COUNTRY WITH MUCH TO OFFER

France has built its reputation on a long and glorious history. Under the Bourbon kings in the eighteenth century, France was known as "the great nation." Under Napoléon I in the early nineteenth century, France conquered most of western and central Europe and spread the republican ideals of the French Revolution. Since the end of World War II in 1945, France has worked hard to restore its industry and economy. To replenish its population, it opened its door to immigration, leading it to become one of the most diverse countries in Europe.

France has long boasted a sophisticated culture, as well as a vibrant artistic and literary tradition. The nation's illustrious history, combined with its modern sense of culture and glamour, have made it one of the most popular destinations in the world.

STATUE OF LIBERTY

Most people know about the Statue of Liberty, which serves as a symbol of freedom, on Liberty Island in the harbor off New York City. The French government, with the assistance of small donations from US citizens, presented the statue to the United States as a symbol of international friendship in 1886. But many people are surprised to learn that two similar statues exist in Paris. A smaller version is located on Paris's Swan Island in the Seine River. Americans living in Paris donated it to the city in 1889 in gratitude. The other statue, erected in 1861, stands in Luxembourg Gardens, on the left bank of the city. The sculptor, Frédéric-Auguste Bartholdi, used it to help prepare for creating the larger statue that would be placed on Liberty Island. Other replicas of Lady Liberty also exist elsewhere in the world.

Political Boundaries of France

SNAPSHOT

Official name: French Republic (French: République Française)

Capital city: Paris

Form of government: republic

Title of leader: president (head of state); prime minister (head of government)

Currency: euro

Population (July 2011 est.): 64,768,389
World rank: 21

Size: 248,429 square miles (643,427 sq km)
World rank: 42

Official language: French

Official religion: None

Per capita GDP (2010, US dollars): $33,300
World rank: 40

CHAPTER 2

GEOGRAPHY: JEWEL OF WESTERN EUROPE

From snowcapped mountains to balmy coastlines, France's size and location make it home to a diverse range of geographic features and climates. In the mountains, the weather is extremely cold during the winter months, and large amounts of snow make ideal conditions for winter sports. Along the Mediterranean shore, mild winters and hot summers are the norm. In between, much of the country enjoys temperate conditions.

France boasts the largest area of any country in western Europe. France consists of 248,429 square miles (643,427 sq km), making it the forty-second-largest country in the world.[1] Metropolitan France, the term used to describe the country without its former colonies and other territories, is slightly larger than the state of Texas.

The Méribel Resort is located in the world's largest lift-linked ski area, in the French Alps.

On the western side, France is bordered by the Bay of Biscay. The English Channel and the countries of Belgium and Luxembourg border France on the north, and the Mediterranean Sea and country of Monaco lie along France's southern border. The country borders Germany, Italy, and Switzerland to the east, while Andorra and Spain are to the south. Within these borders lies a country of diverse climate and geography, from mountains to seaside.

THE COMPLETE FRANCE

In addition to France's European land, it also controls four non-European areas that have the same political status as Metropolitan France: French Guiana in northern South America, between Brazil and Suriname; Guadeloupe, located in the Caribbean islands; Martinique, also in the Caribbean; and Réunion, an island off the coast of southern Africa. Before the 1960s, France also controlled the countries that make up North Africa and much of sub-Saharan Africa, as well as Indochina. All these countries won their freedom, but the sub-Saharan countries remain associated with France in the French Union.

CLIMATE

Most of France enjoys a temperate climate, with extreme cold occurring only high in the mountains. The nation's climate is different in each of its four regions.

Western France has an oceanic climate, which is characterized by narrow temperature changes and plentiful rainfall. Oceanic summers are cool, and winters are chilly but not extremely cold. Rain falls in this region approximately half the year, peaking in the summer months.

Most of east and central France has a continental climate. The summers and winters vary more in temperature than they do in western France. The continental region experiences less rain than the oceanic climate. On average, the region receives 24 inches (60.7 cm) of rain annually.[2]

In continental France, the climate is influenced by three winds, known as la Bise, le Mistral, and le Tramontain. La Bise is a dry, easterly wind that comes from central Europe. It is a wind of extremes: in the winter, it can be extremely cold, while in the summer, it can bring very hot temperatures. When la Bise moves south, down to the Provence region, it becomes le Mistral. This is a dry wind and can last for weeks. During the winter, le Mistral can be very cold. When la Bise wind goes around or over the Massif Central plateau and heads toward the Mediterranean Sea, it becomes le Tramontain, a cold, dry wind.

In the Alps and other high elevations, the climate is categorized as mountainous. The higher the elevation, the colder the temperatures. In the summer, the average temperature is relatively mild, while winters are wet and cold. The amount of precipitation increases with the elevation. In the higher elevations, much of the precipitation is snow. In some locations, snow may fall 50 days out of the year.[3]

France has approximately 1,988 miles (3,200 km) of coastline.

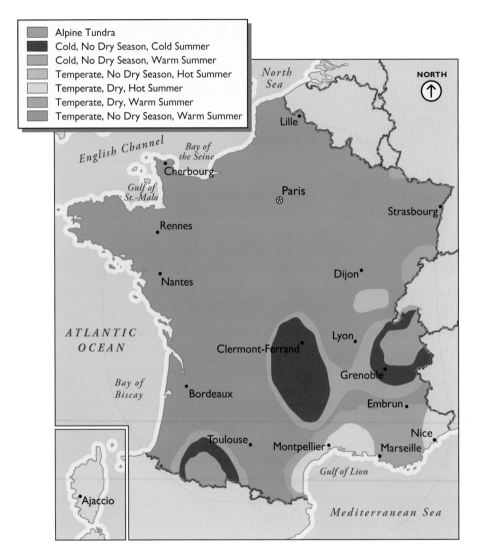

Legend:
- Alpine Tundra
- Cold, No Dry Season, Cold Summer
- Cold, No Dry Season, Warm Summer
- Temperate, No Dry Season, Hot Summer
- Temperate, Dry, Hot Summer
- Temperate, Dry, Warm Summer
- Temperate, No Dry Season, Warm Summer

NORTH

North Sea

English Channel

Bay of the Seine

Lille

Cherbourg

Gulf of St.-Malo

Paris

Strasbourg

Rennes

Nantes

Dijon

ATLANTIC OCEAN

Lyon

Clermont-Ferrand

Grenoble

Bay of Biscay

Bordeaux

Embrun

Nice

Toulouse

Montpellier

Marseille

Gulf of Lion

Ajaccio

Mediterranean Sea

Climate of France

France's southern coastline has a Mediterranean climate, which is characterized by hot summers, mild and sunny winters, and little rain. The region experiences many more days of sun than rain, although occasional severe thunderstorms strike in summertime.

TOPOGRAPHY

Just as France has different climates, it also has varied topography. Most of the north and west of the country is plains. Mountains lie in the east and the south, making these regions popular destinations for skiers, snowboarders, and other vacationers. The most notable of the mountain ranges are the Pyrenees in the south and the Alps in the east. France's highest point is Mont Blanc, in the Alps, which rises 15,771 feet (4,807 m) above sea level.[4] In northern France is the Langres Plateau, where elevations reach more than 1,500 feet (450 m).[5] This area is one of the most heavily forested in the country.

Some of the climatic and topographical traits that make France an attractive place to live and visit can also create natural hazards. Among those hazards are flooding, avalanches, midwinter windstorms, drought, and, in the south near the Mediterranean Sea, forest fires.

The snow-capped peaks of Mont Blanc are reflected in an Alpine lake.

FRANCE'S RIVERS

France's rivers are important to industry, commerce, and tourism. The country has hundreds of rivers and smaller streams, but among the best known are the Loire, the Seine, the Garonne, and the Rhône.

The Loire is the longest river in France, flowing for 634 miles (1,020 km).[6] The river begins in Ardèche, an area of south-central France, on Mount Gerbier-de-Jonc in the Cévennes mountain range, and it empties into the Atlantic Ocean. The Loire also forms the southwest border of Burgundy. Among the most famous cities of the Loire valley is Chartres, home of the Chartres Cathedral, a popular tourist attraction. The river is used for transportation and for recreation, and more than 12 miles (20 km) have been designated a protected nature preserve.[7]

STORMY WEATHER

France was one of several countries worldwide that experienced unusual weather disasters or disturbances in 2010. In February, western and central France were hit by a storm dubbed Xynthia, which had hurricane-force winds. This fierce storm forced many people from their homes permanently. In April, the country experienced record heat, followed by snow in May, an unusual occurrence for that season. And in June, flash floods struck Provence, killing 20 and causing more damage than had occurred in the area for two centuries.

AVERAGE TEMPERATURES AND RAINFALL

Region (City)	Average January Temperature Minimum/ Maximum	Average July Temperature Minimum/Maximum	Average Rainfall January/July
North and Northwestern (Cherbourg)	39.2/46.4°F (4/8°C)	57/66°F (14/19°C)	4.3/2.2 inches (10.9/5.5 cm)
Southwestern (Bourdeaux)	35.6/48.2°F (2/9°C)	57/77°F (14/25°C)	3.5/2.2 inches (9.0/5.6 cm)
Central and Eastern (Paris)	33.8/42.8°F (1/6°C)	59/77°F (15/25°C)	2.2/2.3 inches (5.6/5.9 cm)
Mediterranean Coast and Corsica (Ajaccio)	37.4/55.4°F (3/13°C)	61/81°F (16/27°C)	3.0/0.4 inches (7.6/1.0 cm)
Mountainous (Embrun)	23/41°F (−5/5°C)	54/79°F (12/26°C)	1.9/1.9 inches (4.9/4.8 cm)[9]

The Seine River originates near Dijon, in the Langres Plateau, and flows for 485 miles (780 km) before emptying into the English Channel.[8] It is a major commercial waterway for ships entering and leaving France.

Garonne River in Toulouse

The Seine flows through Paris, dividing the city into the Left Bank, *la Rive Gauche*, and the Right Bank, *la Rive Droite*.

Beginning on the Aneto Peak in the Pyrenees, the Garonne flows 357 miles (575 km) through northern Spain and into southwest France before emptying into the Gironde estuary in the Atlantic Ocean.[10] The Garonne is important to inland shipping, especially for ships and barges that transport agricultural goods from southern France to the Atlantic Ocean. Among the cities along this river is Toulouse.

The Rhône is one of the most important rivers in Europe. It is also the site of the lowest point in France, the Rhône River delta, at 6.5 feet (2 m) below sea level.[11] The river begins at the Rhône Glacier in the Swiss Alps and flows for 505 miles (813 km) before reaching the southwest corner of France and emptying into the Mediterranean Sea.[12] Historically, the Rhône has provided an important trade route from Europe to Mediterranean ports. Lyon, Avignon, and Arles are some of the chief cities that developed along the Rhône River.

CITIES AND RÉGIONS

For administrative purposes, Metropolitan France is divided into 22 *régions*, or provinces. The régions are further divided into 96 departments. France's largest cities are Paris, Marseille, Lyon, and Toulouse.

Paris, located in the Île-de-France région, is the country's capital and by far the largest city. More than 2.2 million people lived within the

Geography of France

borders of Paris as of 2011, and several million more live in the Île-de-France area just outside it.[13] Paris is home to some of France's most popular tourist attractions, including the Louvre, the Eiffel Tower, and the Arc de Triomphe.

Located in the Provence région, Marseille is the second-largest city in France, with a population of 1.5 million.[14] Bordering the Mediterranean Sea, it is the country's largest seaport.

France is shaped roughly like a hexagon.

Lyon is the capital of the Rhône-Alpes région of France and has a population of 1.5 million.[15] Historically, it was known for its silk-weaving industry, but today its major industries are banking and the production of chemicals, pharmaceuticals, and biotechnology. Lyon is also a popular tourist spot, because of its rich history and reputation for gourmet food. During World War II, when Paris fell under Nazi control, Lyon became the center of the Resistance, a movement in which small groups of French civilians conducted sabotage and surveillance activities to drive the Germans from their homeland.

Toulouse is located on the Garonne and has a population of 437,100.[16] This city is home to many aerospace industries, some French owned and some jointly owned by several countries in the European Union. Churches, antiques, and museums are popular among visitors to Toulouse.

A view of the Gorges de Daluis in the south of France

CHAPTER 3

ANIMALS AND NATURE: PRESERVING ECOSYSTEMS

One of France's most famous—or at least, most seen—animals is also one of its national emblems: the Gallic rooster, or *le coq gaulois* (also known as a cockerel). The name of the bird comes from the Latin *gallus*, which means both "resident of Gaul" and "rooster." The rooster was recognized as a warning symbol and a sign of victory in the Bible. Jesus warned

NO ROOSTER FOR NAPOLÉON

After Napoléon I crowned himself emperor in 1804, he did not think a rooster was the appropriate emblem of the world's greatest power. "The rooster has no power. He cannot be the image of an empire the likes of France," Napoléon reportedly remarked.[1] At that point, the Gallic rooster was replaced by an eagle as the symbol of France.

The Gallic rooster is the unofficial symbol of France.

that one of his disciples would betray him before the rooster crowed three times the next morning. Its crowing also represents the victory of morning over night and good over evil.

Although the Gallic rooster does not represent a specific rooster, its importance as a symbol is based on these and similar ideas about roosters. The bird served as a religious symbol in the Middle Ages. During the Renaissance, it began to represent France on coins, and its role as a symbolic representation of the nation grew. During the French Revolution, it became even more ingrained as a national symbol. The rooster was often placed on the flagpoles of regimental flags. But when Napoléon came to power, he replaced the Gallic rooster with an eagle.

Although the Gallic rooster is not the official symbol of France, it has appeared on the country's seal since 1848. It also appears as a symbolic image on coins and stamps and on the international uniforms of French sports teams.

GENETS

In many places in the world, the genet, which is indigenous to France, has been domesticated and made a pet. Resembling a cat physically, the genet has a playful and inquisitive personality similar to that of a kitten. While the genet can use its claws for climbing or holding onto food, it does not use them as weapons while fighting. Genets can be trained to use a litter box and to get along with other pets, such as cats and dogs.

FRANCE'S LESS-FAMOUS ANIMALS

Many of the animals that live in France can also be found in other countries in western Europe—for example, rodents such as the red squirrel, muskrat, rabbit, and hare. Another rodent, the edible dormouse (also called a loir), is common throughout the country. Among France's predatory animals are the fox, wolf, and genet, a catlike animal related to the civet. Wild boar can be found in the country, and red, roe, and fallow deer live in heavily forested areas. The marshlands of Camargue in southern France are home to the semi-wild Camargue horses.

The genet is a catlike animal that is commonly domesticated as a pet.

Other animals indigenous to France include the raccoon dog, coypu (which resembles a brown rat), martens, and midwife toad. There are few reptiles in France.

Some of France's more rare animals are found in the Alps and the Pyrenees. A rare type of goat-antelope species called the chamois lives in these mountain ranges. Alpine marmots live in the treetops of the Alps and jump from tree to tree, eating leaves. The Alpine ibex, which lives above the forest line in the Alps, is listed as endangered after almost being hunted to extinction. The brown bear and the Pyrenees lynx live high in the Pyrenees mountain range.

France is home to many breeds of birds. Flamingos, herons, and egrets are among the birds that make the Mediterranean region their home. More common birds—such as ducks, geese, and thrushes—migrate to France for the winter and then return to their homes in the north when the temperatures begin to warm.

THE EDIBLE DORMOUSE

The edible dormouse has long been a food source, and that is how the name developed. Ancient Romans raised the animals in pits or containers that somewhat resembled hamster cages. Consumption of edible dormice has diminished significantly in France, as nutritional standards have improved, but the animal is still considered a delicacy in the country of Slovenia.

Flamingos wade in a swamp in Camargue, France.

ENDANGERED SPECIES IN FRANCE

According to the International Union for Conservation of Nature (IUCN), France is home to the following numbers of species that are categorized by the organization as Critically Endangered, Endangered, or Vulnerable:

Mammals	9
Birds	7
Reptiles	4
Amphibians	2
Fishes	40
Mollusks	62
Other Invertebrates	29
Plants	15
Total	168[2]

Fishing is a popular recreational activity, and travel companies will even arrange a vacation around fishing for carp. The waters off France are home to several species of whales, including the white whale, the humpback whale, and the northern right whale, which is endangered.

DANGERS TO ANIMALS

As France's population and industry have grown, deforestation has caused a decline in the number of native animals—especially the larger ones, which require more resources to sustain life. When deforestation occurs, a forested area is taken over for agriculture, industry, or housing. Sometimes, animals native to the affected area can be relocated. That may not be possible for some animals, however, and certain species fail to thrive once moved.

In addition to urbanization, hunting has also reduced the numbers of some animals. Several types of deer have been affected, including red, roe, and Corsican deer. In addition, hunting has reduced the populations of ibex, brown bears, marmots, and lynx.

The French government is not blind to the dangers facing many of its animals. It has initiated breeding programs, which have proven somewhat successful in increasing the populations of storks and chamois. Legal hunting continues of some diminishing species, however.

French farmers use dogs and sound machines to keep wolves away from livestock.

PLANT LIFE

The diversity of climate and elevation provides a wide variety of plant life in France. Twenty-nine percent of the country's land is covered to some extent with forests, and that area has increased since 1990. In some cases, the increase has been caused by reforestation projects. In other cases, new lands have been designated as forests.

In the high Alps and Pyrenees, plant life is limited. Only small amounts of lichen and moss are able to survive at such high altitudes and

Vineyards near Fuissé, Burgundy, France

extremely cold temperatures. The few plants that thrive there must be able to establish themselves in sheltered areas.

In the north of France, between the snowline and the timberline, the amount of vegetation increases. Much of this area is covered by pasture, which provides summer grazing for sheep and cattle. These pasture areas are bordered by coniferous forests, where spruce, pine, and fir trees, among others, can be found. Beyond are oak, chestnut, beech, and other deciduous trees. In the middle of France, lavender, juniper, and heath cover the limestone plateaus of the Massif Central region. Larch, beech, and Norway maple trees are also found there.

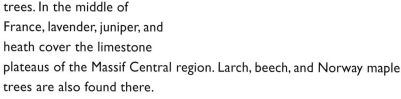

NATIONAL PARKS

France has nine national parks that have been set aside to preserve the country's natural flora and fauna. They are Vanoise (1963), Port-Cros (1963), Pyrenees (1967), Cévennes (1970), Ecrins (1973), Mercantour (1979), Guadeloupe (1989), Réunion Island (2007), and French Guiana (2007). Together they cover approximately 8 percent of French territory.[3]

The plant life in France's Mediterranean region must be able to withstand much warmer temperatures and droughts than the vegetation found elsewhere in the country. Among the trees that grow here are the evergreen oak, cork oak, pine, and sweet chestnut. A dense shrub called the maquis covers much of the rural area of Roussillon. Provence, where many of France's vineyards and fruit trees are grown, is the home of the garigue, another shrub.

Flowers are popular in France. Many people grow them in home gardens, and they are often key components of public and private landscaping. The stylized lily is the country's national flower.

DANGERS TO PLANT LIFE

Urbanization has led to environmental damage to France's plant life, as it has elsewhere in the world. Some of the country's most significant environmental issues are water pollution caused by urban waste and agricultural runoff and acid rain, a by-product of the air pollution caused by vehicle and industry carbon emissions. Yet compared with neighboring Germany, where much of the Black Forest has died, France is comparatively healthy in ecological terms.

Brown bears have not been seen in the French Alps since the 1930s.

The French government has tried to fight some of these problems. The government has been an active participant in programs aimed at domestic and international conservation. For example, France signed the Kyoto Protocol on April 29, 1998, joining nations worldwide in an effort to reduce global warming. The country has also established national parks, regional parks, and nature reserves to protect animals and plants. Moreover, France has made reforestation a priority.

A coniferous forest in the Aquitaine région of France

in Gaul. King Clovis established the Merovingian dynasty, accepted Christianity, and aligned the kingdom with the Roman Catholic Church.

THE KINGS

The years that followed saw many men rule France. Transitions of power often involved conflict among local feudal rulers, and the land was divided following battles. The region became more stable, however, after Pope Leo III crowned Charlemagne emperor of the Western Roman Empire on December 25, 800 CE. Charlemagne's empire would grow to include most of western Europe, which his son, Louis the Pious, ruled following his death. After Louis died in 840, the land was divided among Louis's three sons in a treaty signed at Verdun in 843.

The long-lasting Capetian dynasty began when Hugh Capet was crowned in 987. In 1328, the death of King Charles IV set off a series of conflicts with England that became known as the Hundred Years' War (1337–1453). The conflict started when English king Edward III made a claim to the French throne, based on the fact that his French mother was related to Charles IV. As internal power struggles and warfare occurred over the next century, the French lost territory in the west and north, including Paris.

In 1422, English king Henry V died, leaving only an infant heir. Charles VII of France seized the opportunity to reclaim territory. He was aided by Joan of Arc, who rallied French troops to resist the English. Joan was burned at the stake in 1431, but over the next several decades,

JOAN OF ARC

Joan of Arc, also called the Maid of Orléans (circa 1412–May 30, 1431), is a much-beloved figure and one of France's patron saints. She claimed to have received divine guidance and used it to lead the French Army to victories during the Hundred Years' War. Her guidance in those battles helped lead to the coronation of Charles VII. Joan was later captured by the Burgundians and sold to the English. At age 19, she was tried by a religious court for heresy (unacceptable religious beliefs), found guilty, and burned at the stake. In 1456, Pope Callixtus III declared her a martyr after examining the records of the trial and concluding that she had been unjustly convicted and executed. In 1920, Joan was raised to sainthood.

Charles VII was able to reclaim much of the nation's lost territory.

FRANCE THE COLONIZER

Because France spent several centuries involved in European warfare, the nation lagged behind Spain and Portugal in the race to colonize the New World. Interest increased, however, when a French privateer captured a Spanish ship carrying gold and silver.

Spurred by the desire to increase his wealth, King Francis I decided to send out two navigators in search of a Northwest Passage to the Orient in 1523. This marked the beginning of the first French colonial empire. Although Giovanni da Verrazzano did not find the rumored passage, he did claim portions of North America on behalf of France.

An engraving depicts Joan of Arc in battle.

In 1534 and 1535, Jacques Cartier made two voyages across the Atlantic. On the latter trip, he sailed up the Saint Lawrence River, reaching the site of what would later become Montreal, Canada.

One of France's largest claims in the Americas, made in 1682, was Louisiana—at that time, a vast area encompassing much of the land through which the Mississippi River and its tributaries flowed. This conquest gave the French a trading stronghold in the Americas that reached from the Mississippi Delta at New Orleans to Canada.

Once the French got a taste of colonization, they did not limit their conquests to the New World. French colonies were also established in the West Indies, South America, Senegal, India, and Saint-Domingue, which is today Haiti. In the eighteenth century, when sugar became a hugely profitable crop, the sugar islands of the Caribbean contributed a great deal to French prosperity.

DECLINE OF THE MONARCHY

When Louis XIV ascended the throne at age five in 1643, France was the dominant power in Europe. But during his 72-year rule, Louis XIV depleted the national treasury by engaging in a series of wars to gain territory and by building an extravagant palace at Versailles to undermine the power of the nobles.

A statue of King Louis XIV in Versailles, France

THE GRAND CENTURY

Many civilizations have had periods in which the focus was on extravagance. In France, the period between 1598 and 1715 is considered its "grand century." During that time, the monarchy held absolute power and indulged in several forms of excess. For example, King Louis XIV entertained princes and members of the high nobility with lavish parties at the Palace of Versailles. By inviting the nobles to be his guests, the king also undermined their independence and made it less likely they would overthrow him. In addition, King Louis XIV carried out numerous wars, which were expensive.

In the end, paying for Louis XIV's extravagances almost brought France to financial ruin. The enduring legacy of this period, however, is a rich collection of architecture, literature, and music.

His grandson, Louis XV (who ruled from 1715 to1774), continued this trend with the expensive Seven Years' War, a complicated conflict involving all the great powers of Europe. The part of this conflict that occurred across the Atlantic was called the French and Indian War, and it involved France battling Great Britain for control of the North American colonies. The war ended in 1763 with the Treaty of Paris, which required France to give up much of its control over the area south of Canada and east of the Mississippi.

Before leaving for America to join the American Revolution, a general is interviewed by Louis XVI and Marie Antoinette.

During the American Revolution (1775–1783), France fought on the side of the colonies as a way of carrying on the struggle against England. But being involved in this conflict nearly bankrupted France. In addition, supporting the American Revolution spread ideas about democracy among the French people.

At this time, unrest was growing in France among the Third Estate (a class of commoners) about the class system, which reserved power and position for a small elite class of aristocrats. The merchants in the port cities resented the fact that they could not have the level of social or political recognition that fit their wealth and education. And while French peasants owned more land than the agricultural classes elsewhere in Europe, they resented having to pay taxes, called seigneurial dues, to noble landlords. In May 1789, Louis XVI convened a meeting to decide on fiscal reforms with representatives of the clergy, the nobility, and the Third Estate. When a disagreement arose over the Third Estate's role in the process, they broke away. Declaring themselves a National Assembly, this group of commoners set out to develop a new constitution.

On the night of July 14, 1789, a mob stormed the Bastille, a prison fortress in Paris. This signified the beginning of the French Revolution. Few prisoners were actually held there, but to the Third Estate, the Bastille represented what they viewed as royal tyranny. In August, the

France began using the guillotine for executions in 1792.

A mob storms the Bastille on July 14, 1789.

National Assembly ended the class system and approved the Declaration of the Rights of Man and of the Citizen, which guaranteed rights and equality for all. King Louis XVI was overthrown, imprisoned, and finally executed in 1793 along with his wife, Queen Marie Antoinette.

In 1792, a new National Convention abolished the monarchy and declared France a republic. The revolutionaries in power enacted a series of reforms—from taxing the rich to confiscating property of the former nobility. Many members of the nobility fled abroad. For several years, the revolution fed on itself, with each group of leaders denouncing their predecessors.

In 1795, the National Convention established a more moderate government called the Directory, which included a two-house parliament and a five-man executive. Nevertheless, the Directory suffered from a weak executive branch and failed to defend France successfully against its many foreign enemies.

Napoléon I, a member of the minor Corsican nobility who had become a brilliant army officer, seized power in 1799. After raising a large army through a draft and leading France in a series of successful wars, he crowned himself emperor in 1804. During his ten-year reign, Napoléon promoted social mobility and made careers open to people with talents.

Napoléon I

THE FRENCH EMPIRE

Napoléon I's wars against the other European powers took place not only in Europe but also in other parts of the world. Napoléon introduced many of the administrative reforms of the French Revolution in the countries he conquered and opened the way to a career based on talent, rather than birth. The Napoleonic Wars can also be seen, however, as a continuation of the long eighteenth-century struggle that pitted France against Great Britain.

THE REPUBLICS

France is a republic, a form of government with elected representatives. The governments that have been in place in France throughout its history are often referred to as the First Republic, the Second Republic, and so on. The numerical designation refers to the constitution under which the country was governed. France's most recent constitution, enacted in 1958, is the fifth one, which makes the current government the Fifth Republic.

Conflict also took place in Egypt, the United States, and parts of Latin America. In 1803, Napoléon was forced to sell the Louisiana area to the United States, and this transaction, known as the Louisiana Purchase, doubled the area of the new American nation. The same year, a slave revolt on the rich sugar-producing island of Haiti undermined French rule there.

The aristocratic powers of Europe feared

that an expanded France would spread its revolutionary message and undermine monarchies that ruled by divine right. In 1812, Napoléon's army suffered huge losses and was turned back in its attempt to invade Russia. Then, after Prussia reformed its army, the European powers combined to drive Napoléon into exile.

After the Congress of Vienna in 1815, the Bourbon monarchy was restored. The restored Bourbon kings generally followed a cautious foreign policy. But in 1830, France embarked on a new colonial venture by taking control of Algeria. Revolutions took place in 1830 and 1848, the latter leading to a short-lived republic.

In 1852, a nephew of Napoléon I then took over and ruled as Napoléon III. In the 1860s, Napoléon III, hoping to revive the glory of his uncle, tried to conquer Mexico. Between 1858 and 1864, Napoléon III also carried out a number of campaigns against local rulers in Indochina, where France had long been involved in protecting Catholic missionaries. Cambodia asked to be made a French protectorate in 1863. After the defeat of Napoléon III in the Franco-Prussian war in 1871, France became a republic. France did not complete the conquest of northern Indochina until the period from 1884 to 1887.

After a conference of the European powers set the rules for African expansion in 1884–85, French explorers penetrated large areas of sub-Saharan Africa and established protectorates there. France eventually

Charles De Gaulle holds the world record for surviving the most assassination attempts (32).

dominated almost the entire northern coast of Africa, along with sub-Saharan Africa, Syria and Lebanon, and Indochina.

FRANCE AND THE WORLD WARS

World War I broke out in the summer of 1914 following the assassination of Austrian Archduke Franz Ferdinand. Germany declared war on France on August 3 after France mobilized its troops to help Belgium. On September 5, France joined forces with Great Britain and Russia to form the Triple Entente and defend itself against the Central powers: Germany and Austria.

The German armed forces moved rapidly through Belgium with the goal of capturing Paris before the Russians could mobilize. But the French stopped the German drive. After the front stabilized in northern France, the French and their British allies faced the German enemy along a line of trenches several hundred miles long. The deadlock on the western front continued, with great loss of life, until 1918, when US troops succeeded in coming to the aid of the Allies and broke the stalemate.

Although most of France was saved, parts of the country's north were devastated. The residents of those areas were subjected to the brutality of the German troops, although they were not deported for slave labor, as some Belgians were. As the Germans retreated, they

French troops peer over an embankment, part of an Allied firing line, battling German forces, during World War I.

flooded the mines and destroyed the factories. The area needed to be rebuilt, and France would have to fund the project unless Germany could be forced to pay reparations.

On November 11, 1918, an armistice was signed that ended World War I. But the principal Allies disagreed about many aspects of it, including reparations, borders, and limitations on the German army. To address those issues, the Treaty of Versailles was signed on June 28, 1919. Germany was ordered to pay reparations, but it struggled against doing so for many years. Although France was able to restore its devastated regions and made progress in industrialization in the 1920s, Germany remained the stronger power.

In an attempt to avoid future attacks, France worked during the 1930s to establish an elaborate system of eastern border defenses called the Maginot Line. And as Germany broke loose from the military limitations of the Treaty of Versailles, France made a series of alliances intended to prevent its defeat in a future conflict. Those efforts proved pointless, however, for several reasons. Russia had become a Communist nation, the Union of Soviet Socialist Republics (USSR), following a revolution in 1917, and Great Britain and the United States had decided to limit their commitments on the European continent.

In June 1940, during the early days of World War II, German troops and tanks defeated the French army in less than six weeks by going around the Maginot Line and cutting through the Ardennes Mountains.

Once again, France was occupied. The Germans divided the country in two: a northern section ruled by the Nazis and a southern section governed by the regime of Marshal Pétain, a French World War I hero.

After the Allies invaded North Africa in November 1942, the Nazis took over all of France. French factories and mines were redirected to the German war effort. Also, hundreds of thousands of French men were forced to labor under terrible conditions in Germany. All foreign Jews, and eventually many French Jews, were sent to concentration camps in Poland. US and British forces liberated France in 1944, but the country again faced the painful task of social and economic reconstruction.

THE RESISTANCE

After the fall of France in June 1940, an underground anti-Nazi movement emerged that became known as the French Resistance. By 1943, a number of these groups had unified to become the National Council of the Resistance. Members of the French Resistance assisted the Allies by gathering intelligence, disrupting the supply and communication lines of Germans, and attacking the Germans when possible. Resistance-gathered intelligence played a role in the days that led up to D-day, June 6, 1944, and Germany's subsequent defeat.

THE FOURTH AND FIFTH REPUBLICS

The formal end of World War II did not bring an end to France's problems. General Charles de Gaulle set up a provisional government

Outgoing President René Coty greets newly elected President Charles de Gaulle, *right,* **in 1958.**

in October 1944, and in the spring of 1946, a parliamentary government known as the Fourth Republic was elected based on a new constitution. Despite efforts to revive the French economy with the help of US aid, the office of the president, then held by René Coty, proved too weak to provide stability. The government finally collapsed on May 13, 1958.

To avoid a potential civil war, de Gaulle carried out a bloodless coup d'état and was elected president. He revised the constitution and created the Fifth Republic, based on a strong executive. De Gaulle managed to extract France from the colonial struggle in Algeria and to reestablish the country's international importance. Under his leadership, France also came to dominate the European common market, which would eventually be transformed into the European Union. De Gaulle won reelection in 1965, but he resigned when a referendum turned down his plan for 21 regions that would have limited self-governing powers.

De Gaulle's new institutional structure has stood the test of time. As of 2011, five individuals had followed him as president: Georges Pompidou (1969–1974), Valéry Giscard d'Estaing (1974–1981), François Mitterrand (1981–1995), Jacques Chirac (1995–2007), and Nicolas Sarkozy (elected in 2007).

CHAPTER 5

PEOPLE: THE CHANGING FACE OF THE FRENCH

France has 22 régions, and each has characteristics that add variety to the country as a whole. Perhaps the most obvious contribution is language. Although French is the official language and required in school, other dialects are spoken in some rural areas, including Basque, Breton, Caló, Franco-Provençal, and Ligurian. Use of these dialects is declining, however, because of the spread of television and other mass media, and two dialects—Shaudit and Zarphatic—are no longer spoken.

In addition to regional dialects, France's large immigrant population has brought other languages to the country. Among those are Armenian, Assyrian Neo-Aramaic, Central Khmer, Chru, Giáy, Hmong Daw, Kabyle, Lesser Antillean Creole French, Turkish, and Vietnamese.

Friends at a Parisian café

A teacher writes conjugations of the French verb *aller*, which means "to go," on a chalkboard.

YOU SAY IT!

English	French
Hello/Good morning	Bonjour (bohn-ZHOOR)
Good-bye	Au revoir (ohr uh-VWAHR)
Good night	Bonne nuit (bohn NWEET)
Good evening	Bonsoir (bohn-SWAHR)
Please	S'il vous plaît (SEE voo play)
Thank you	Merci (mehr-SEE)
Excuse me	excusez-moi (ex-cooz-ay MWAH)
Yes	Oui (WEE)
No	Non (NOHN)
I don't know.	Je ne sais pas. (Zhun say pah)
I'm hungry.	J'ai faim. (zhay FAM)
Do you speak English?	Parlez-vous anglais? (par-lay-voo ahn-GLAY)
How are you?	Comment allez-vous? (COH-moh TAH-lay VOO)

While the study and use of other languages is tolerated somewhat, the French government takes its official language very seriously. In 1635, Cardinal Richelieu, minister to King Louis XIII, established the French Academy to oversee the use of the French language. The academy was suspended during the French Revolution, but Napoléon I restored it in 1803.

The primary role of the French Academy is to regulate the French language. It determines what is acceptable grammar and vocabulary, creates new words, and revises the meanings of existing words to reflect

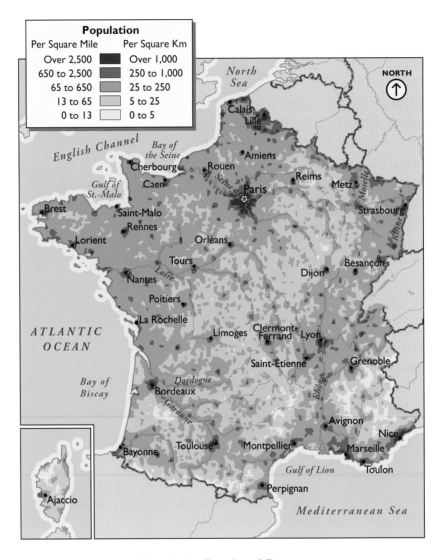

Population

Per Square Mile	Per Square Km
Over 2,500	Over 1,000
650 to 2,500	250 to 1,000
65 to 650	25 to 250
13 to 65	5 to 25
0 to 13	0 to 5

NORTH

North Sea

English Channel

Bay of the Seine

Calais
Lille
Amiens
Cherbourg
Rouen
Reims
Metz
Caen
Seine
Paris
Strasbourg
Moselle
Brest
Saint-Malo
Rennes
Orléans
Lorient
Tours
Besançon
Nantes
Loire
Dijon
Poitiers
La Rochelle
Limoges
Clermont-Ferrand
Lyon
Saint-Étienne
Grenoble
Gulf of St.-Malo

ATLANTIC OCEAN

Bay of Biscay

Dordogne
Bordeaux
Garonne
Rhône
Avignon
Nice
Bayonne
Toulouse
Montpellier
Marseille
Toulon
Perpignan
Gulf of Lion

Mediterranean Sea

Ajaccio

Population Density of France

changes in language. It also tries to lessen the influence of English on French. When an English word threatens to make its way into common usage among the French, the academy seeks to find a French equivalent. If one does not exist, the academy creates a new one.

POPULATION DISTRIBUTION

As in most industrialized countries, the population in France is concentrated in its cities. In 2010, 85 percent of the French population lived in urban areas.[1] France's largest cities are Paris, Marseille, Lyon, and Toulouse.

France's urban population has increased steadily, as people have moved to urban areas to take jobs, especially higher-paying ones. The nation's mountainous regions continue to lose their population more quickly than other areas, as good jobs have become increasingly difficult to find.

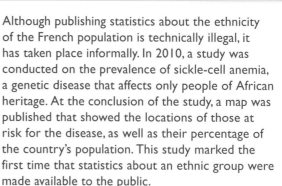

FRENCH ETHNIC STATISTICS

Although publishing statistics about the ethnicity of the French population is technically illegal, it has taken place informally. In 2010, a study was conducted on the prevalence of sickle-cell anemia, a genetic disease that affects only people of African heritage. At the conclusion of the study, a map was published that showed the locations of those at risk for the disease, as well as their percentage of the country's population. This study marked the first time that statistics about an ethnic group were made available to the public.

DEMOGRAPHICS

Most French people are of either Celt or Latin descent. Other ethnicities are represented, as well, including Teutonic, Slavic, North African, Indochinese, and Basque. Small groups of Flemings, Catalans, Germans, Armenians, Gypsies, Russians, and Poles are also found within the French population.

"Francophones" are people who speak fluent French.

Since the end of World War I, France has maintained an open immigration policy, for the most part. Authorities encouraged immigration to help rebuild the population after World War I and World War II, when more than 1.5 million French people lost their lives. The deaths of young men, in particular, had left the country's fertility rate quite low. Immigrants also helped fill jobs that were created when the economy rebounded, since women were slow to enter the workforce.

Over the years, tension has developed between native-born French people and members of some immigrant groups. Laws regarding non-European immigration have tightened slightly, although citizens of European Union countries can work in France under the Schengen Agreement. According to the French Institute of National Statistics, in 2004–2005, 4.9 million immigrants were living in France. That represents 8 percent of the country's population.[2] France receives large numbers of immigrants from Algeria, Portugal, Morocco, Italy, Spain, Tunisia, Turkey, Germany, the United Kingdom, Belgium, and Poland.

Shoppers and commuters fill a street in Bordeaux in southwestern France.

The French constitution specifically indicates that the country must be secular. While the word *secular* usually refers to a lack of religious connection, in the context of the French constitution, it means that a French citizen is French first; whatever ethnic or religious affiliation he or she may claim is not important. To emphasize the importance of maintaining secularism, French law forbids the compilation of official statistics on ethnicity.

Sixty-five percent of the French population is between the ages of 15 and 64.[3] The average person in France has a life expectancy of 81.09 years; the average life expectancy for women is 84.44, and for men, it is 77.91.[4]

DEMOGRAPHICS BY AGE

Based on 2010 estimates, the French population can be divided into these age groups:[5]

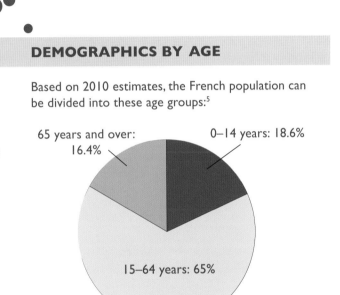

65 years and over: 16.4%

0–14 years: 18.6%

15–64 years: 65%

RELIGION IN FRANCE

Religion has been an important part of French life for centuries. The French constitution guarantees freedom of religion, and there is no official religion. Between 83 and 88 percent of the population indicate they are Roman Catholic.[6] Considering the country's long history and the close association between many of the monarchs and popes, the large number of Catholics is no surprise. Two percent of the population identify themselves as Protestant, 1 percent Jewish, and 4 percent unaffiliated. Between 5 and 10 percent indicate they are Muslim, or followers of Islam.[7] Islam is one of the fastest-growing religions in France, which reflects the increasing population of immigrants from Muslim nations.

RELIGION OR CULT?

Religion is considered a private matter in France. In fact, many individuals consider being asked about their religious beliefs an invasion of privacy. To some people in and out of government, the existence of a government-sanctioned report on cults is objectionable, regardless of its intent.

A controversy on the subject of cults has raged since 1995, when the French National Assembly established the Parliamentary Commission on Cults in France. This occurred following the 1995 murder-suicides in southeast France (as well as Switzerland and Canada), which allegedly involved members of the Order of the Solar Temple. The commission was created to determine what constitutes a cult. Various groups were categorized according to their potential threat to members, society, and the state. The commission's first report was issued in 1995, and subsequent reports were released in 1996 and 2006.

SCIENTOLOGY ON TRIAL

Officials of the Church of Scientology were convicted of defrauding recruits in France on October 25, 2009. According to testimony, prospective members gave thousands of dollars to the church because of false statements and promises made by church officials. The Scientology Celebrity Center and its bookshop were fined more than $800,000. Prosecutors originally wanted the courts to order the church to disband. The law that would have allowed this was temporarily changed, however. Because the trial was already in progress when the law was reinstated, it did not apply.

Other religions practiced by the French include Jehovah's Witness, Adventist, Mormon, Sukyo Mahikari, and Soka Gakkai (a branch of Buddhism). The French government's Parliamentary Commission on Cults has identified several groups as cults, including the Universal White Brotherhood, New Acropolis, Church of Scientology, and Universal Alliance (formerly the Universal Christian Church).

Parisians gather on the steps of the Sacred Heart Basilica.

CHAPTER 6
CULTURE: WHERE HISTORIC MEETS CHIC

One of the most famous museums in the world is the Louvre Museum. Located in Paris, the Louvre was built as a fortress in the late twelfth century. It served as a palace until 1682, when King Louis XIV decided he would rather live at the Palace of Versailles. The Louvre then was used to exhibit the royal collection of art. On August 10, 1793, the Louvre opened officially as a museum. Since then, it has been renovated numerous times.

Among the masterpieces housed within the Louvre are Italian artist Leonardo da Vinci's *Mona Lisa*, French artist Eugène Delacroix's *Liberty Leading the People*, and Dutch painter Rembrandt's *Self-Portrait Bareheaded*.

French writer Charles Perrault wrote children's classics *Cinderella* and *Sleeping Beauty*.

The Louvre Museum houses some of the most famous works of art in the world.

ART

Many international art movements began in France. Realism, for example, began as an art and literary movement in 1848 as a reaction to the flourish and idealization of the romantic movement. Realism focused on presenting life as it really was, not as the artist imagined it could be. The primary subjects of realist art and literature were everyday people in their natural surroundings and performing their usual activities. Realism developed a following among landscape painters, as well. Artists of the Barbizon school painted the landscapes they observed as faithfully as possible in two-dimensional form. Among the most famous artists of the realist movement and Barbizon school were Jean-Baptiste Camille Corot, Théodore Rousseau, and Jean-François Millet.

Realism led the way to other art movements, including impressionism, symbolism, postimpressionism, art nouveau, cubism, surrealism, and art deco. Like the

POINTILLISM

One of the most original artistic movements of the nineteenth century is represented by the work of French painter Georges Seurat (1859–1891). Seurat founded the postimpressionist school of painting known as pointillism, in which images are created using small dots. When viewed up close, the subject of the painting appears to be a collection of dots, but from a distance, the image clearly comes into focus. This technique was used to create Seurat's *Sunday Afternoon on the Island of La Grande Jatte* (1884–1886).

realists, some of the followers of these movements tried to present subjects in their natural states. Others, such as cubist and surrealist artist Marcel Duchamp, created works with little resemblance to the real world.

ARCHITECTURE

France has played an important part in the world's architectural history. The first architectural movement to originate in France was the Gothic style, which began in the twelfth century. An important example of this architectural style is the church of Saint-Denis, which was built between 1137 and 1144. Examples of another important style, Rococo, can be seen in both the exterior and interior designs of the Palace of Versailles.

Examples of contemporary architectural styles are also found in France. Among them is the Villa Savoye (1928–1930), outside Paris. It was designed by French-Swiss architect Charles-Édouard Jeanneret, who worked under the name

THE PYRAMID

In 1983, American architect I. M. Pei was awarded a contract to renovate the Louvre. He designed a glass pyramid to stand over a new entrance, which opened on March 30, 1989. The rest of the renovation was complete by 1993. The design was not met with overwhelming approval when first presented, but since its completion, attendance at the museum has increased. The pyramid has also become a modern symbol of the Louvre.

The Palace of Versailles was designed in the Baroque style
during the seventeenth century.

Le Corbusier. Another example of modern French architecture is the new Bibliothèque Nationale, France's national library, designed by Dominique Perrault. It was opened to the public on December 20, 1996.

MUSIC

France's influence on music can be traced back to the tenth century, when a chant-like composition called the organum was developed. By the end of the twelfth century, choral compositions called motets were popular. Between 1100 and 1300, musicians called troubadours traveled the country, especially southern France.

Folk, classical, and popular music are all prevalent in France today. Additionally, each ethnic group has its own form of folk music. In many areas, bagpipes and similar instruments are integral to the folk music. The biniou, used in the instrumental music of Brittany, is similar to the Scottish bagpipes, but the pitch is higher. The accordion and hurdy-gurdy are also important instruments in French folk music.

In the sixteenth and seventeenth centuries, classical music, especially that associated with opera, took hold in France. Eventually, French composers developed their own style, and by the mid-nineteenth century, the nation enjoyed a high era of classical music. Among the best-known French composers of classical music are Hector Berlioz, Lili Boulanger, Claude Debussy, and Maurice Ravel.

In the 1920s, jazz was popular in the clubs of Paris. During the 1930s, Edith Piaf and Charles Trenet drew crowds to nightclubs. The 1950s saw the rise of cabarets, especially in Paris, where people came to hear performers such as Jacques Brel and Serge Gainsbourg.

During the 1960s, pop music became popular in France, especially the music of Johnny Hallyday. Beginning in the 1980s, Les Rita Mitsouko's blend of punk, New Wave, dance, and cabaret became popular in Europe. Electronic music has won a following, and the groups M83 and Phoenix are among those that remain popular.

Hip-hop and rap found their way to France in the 1980s. Although not as popular in France as in the United States, MC Solaar has found some success.

HOLIDAYS

France celebrates several public holidays in addition to regional festivals. The biggest holiday is July 14, *Fête de la Fédération*, known outside of France as Bastille Day. It commemorates the first anniversary of the 1789 storming of the French prison by irate Parisians, which eventually led to the overthrow of the monarchy in the French Revolution. The day is celebrated with parades, art fairs, and parties.

French singer Edith Piaf performs in New York City in the 1950s.

Another significant French holiday is the Carnival of Nice, which occurs there in late winter. Costumed parades, carnivals, and booths featuring food are the major attractions. Near the end of the year, on the third Thursday of November, the yearly uncorking of the first *Beaujolais Nouveau*, a type of red wine, is a cause for much celebration.

On May 1, the country celebrates Labor Day and on May 8, World War II Victory Day. Also in May, the city of Sédan hosts the Medieval Festival of Sédan. During this celebration, residents and visitors are returned to the Middle Ages, complete with knights on horses, falconry, and medieval costumes. Those inclined to do so can stay in a local castle.

A FOOD LOVER'S DELIGHT

Food is one of the cultural elements for which France is best known. Each region has a specialty. In southwest France, rich foods such as duck and truffles are popular. In the northwest, fruits, cheeses, and crepes are favored.

In northeast France, where temperatures can get very cold and some food crops are difficult to grow, dishes are hearty and sometimes considered peasant food. Potatoes, cabbage, and beets are the basis of many of these dishes.

Eastern France, which borders Germany, features foods that are influenced by German cuisine. Pickled cabbage and pork dishes are popular, as are heavy, savory pastries and tarts. This area is also the

A parade of elaborate floats entertains spectators at the Carnival of Nice.

French breads and pastries are on display in a bakery in Metz, a town in northern France.

birthplace of quiche Lorraine, an egg and cheese tart.

The Burgundy region is known for its high-quality beef and wine, and these products often appear in regional dishes. Dijon mustard also comes from this area.

"Light, refined, learned and noble, harmonious and orderly, clear and logical, the cooking of France is, in some strange manner, intimately linked to the genius of her greatest men."[1]

—*Marcel Rouff, French journalist and writer*

The food of southern France is influenced by Spanish cooking and tastes, again reflecting a neighboring cuisine. Dishes are often spicy and include sausage and tomatoes, which are readily available in this region.

Southeast France shares a border with Italy, and so Italian cooking has influenced this region's dishes. Many foods feature olives, olive oil, herbs, tomatoes, and garlic.

SPORTS

Sports are another important part of French culture. Soccer is the most popular sport, followed by tennis, judo, horseback riding, and basketball.

Many French athletes have achieved international success and popularity. Among them are skier Jean-Claude Killy, basketball player Tony

Parker, race car driver Alain Prost, and the late professional wrestler André René Roussimoff, known as André the Giant.

LITERATURE, FILM, AND TELEVISION

France has a long and proud tradition in literature. Many French authors have composed works that have become classics and are read around the world. These include Albert Camus (*The Stranger*), Victor Hugo (*Les Misérables*), Alexandre Dumas (*The Three Musketeers*), Marcel Proust (*Remembrance of Things Past*), Jules Verne (*Around the World in Eighty Days*), and George Sand (*Letters of a Traveler*). Contemporary authors include Chloé Delaume and Nina Bouraoui.

French actors have been featured in films and television all over the world. Some of the best known are Jean Reno, Juliette Binoche, Gérard Depardieu, and Marion Cotillard. French directors, as well, including François Truffaut, Jean Renoir, and Jean-Luc Godard, have influenced world cinema.

Yul Brynner, *left*, presents an Oscar for Best Foreign Language Film to French director François Truffaut in 1974.

CHAPTER 7
POLITICS:
THE FIFTH REPUBLIC

In 2007, when Nicolas Sarkozy was elected president of France, he found himself facing multiple issues, such as immigration, terrorism, and the country's role in the European Union. France was also experiencing serious economic difficulties, like most countries. To prevent the nation's economy from worsening, Sarkozy put into place tax incentives for individuals and businesses. He also reached out to US President Barack Obama, hoping to work with him to fortify both the French and US economies.

Politically, the US and French governments have not always been on friendly terms. When the United States went to war against Iraq in 2003, France opposed the move. For a while, the relationship between the two

A term has been coined for obsessing over President Nicolas Sarkosy: Sarkosis.

French President Nicolas Sarkozy greets supporters in October 2010.

countries was tense. Some in the US government considered France's refusal to support the war as a betrayal. To reflect disapproval of France's position, some restaurants—including the dining room of the US Congress—renamed French fries as "freedom fries."

In recent years, the relationship between France and the United States has improved. President Sarkozy continues to work to improve relations for the benefit of both countries.

SYSTEM OF GOVERNMENT

France is a republic, meaning that the country has an elected chief of state and the government's power lies in its citizens, who choose leaders. The French government is divided into three branches: executive, legislative, and judicial.

STRUCTURE OF THE GOVERNMENT OF FRANCE

Executive Branch		Legislative Branch	Judicial Branch
President	Prime Minister	Senate	Supreme Court of Appeals
Council of Ministers		National Assembly	Constitutional Council
			Council of State

In the executive branch, the president serves as the chief of state. The president is elected to a five-year term by the popular vote of citizens above age 18. The president appoints and shares power with the prime minister, who is the head of the government. The president appoints the members of the Council of Ministers, with the input of the prime minister. Ministries include the Ministry of Transportation, Ministry of Interior, and Ministry of Foreign Affairs, among others. As the needs of the country change, ministries on the council can change. Other presidential duties include receiving foreign ambassadors, referring laws to the Constitutional Court for review, and granting pardons. The president also names most officials, but approval by the parliament is required in most cases.

France's legislative branch consists of a bicameral, or two-level, parliament. The upper house is the 343-member Senate. Metropolitan France and overseas departments are represented by 321 members, and the remaining members represent other French-ruled countries and French individuals living outside the country. Members of the Senate are

THE ELECTORAL COLLEGE

Under a system that uses an electoral college, people do not vote directly for a candidate. Instead, their vote selects an individual who will cast a vote, or votes, on behalf of everyone who voted for that candidate. The number of electoral votes assigned to a state, region, or district depends on its population.

elected to six-year terms by an electoral college. One-third of the Senate seats come up for election every three years.

The lower house of parliament is the National Assembly. Of the 577 members of the National Assembly, 555 represent Metropolitan France, and the remainder act on behalf of departments and dependencies, which are territories under the jurisdiction of other countries. Members of the National Assembly are elected by popular vote. All seats come up for election every five years.

France's judicial branch is comprised of three courts. The Supreme Court of Appeals hears final appeals of civil and criminal judgments. The president appoints judges to this court after receiving nominations from the High Court of the Judiciary. The responsibility of another judicial body, the Constitutional Council, is to make certain that the rules set forth in the constitution are followed. There are nine members of the council: three appointed by the president, three appointed by the president of the National Assembly, and three appointed by the president of the Senate. Another judicial body, the Council of State, provides legal advice to the executive branch and has the final word on matters heard in administrative courts.

France is one of five permanent members of the United Nations Security Council.

The French flag

THE CONSTITUTION OF FRANCE

The authority of the French government is based on the country's current constitution: the Constitution of the Fifth Republic. It was adopted on October 4, 1958, and replaced the constitution of the Fourth Republic, which had been in effect for 12 years.

PREAMBLE TO THE FRENCH CONSTITUTION

The French constitution begins: "The French people solemnly proclaim their attachment to the Rights of Man and the principles of national sovereignty as defined by the Declaration of 1789, confirmed and complemented by the Preamble to the Constitution of 1946, and to the rights and duties as defined in the Charter for the Environment of 2004.

"By virtue of these principles and that of the self-determination of peoples, the Republic offers to the overseas territories which have expressed the will to adhere to them new institutions founded on the common ideal of liberty, equality and fraternity and conceived for the purpose of their democratic development."[1]

The preamble to the constitution reasserts the Declaration of the Rights of Man and of the Citizen, which states that all people have universal rights that are valid regardless of the time and place. This declaration, which dates back to 1789, has been used as the basis of many international human rights proclamations. In addition, the French constitution affirms the separation of powers and national sovereignty and proclaims that government ultimately receives its power from

The French National Assembly meets in the National Assembly building in Paris.

The French National Assembly in session

the citizens through the electoral process.

Among the issues addressed in the constitution are how the president, parliament, and other government authorities are to be selected; what powers belong to the various governmental bodies and what relationship exists among them; and how the constitution can be amended. The ratification of treaties, including those associated with the European Union, is also discussed.

PRESIDENT NICOLAS SARKOZY

Nicolas Sarkozy was born in Paris on January 28, 1955, to Greek and Hungarian immigrant parents. From 1983 to 2002, he served as mayor of Neuilly-sur-Seine. He also served as budget minister and official spokesman for Prime Minister Édouard Balladur from 1993 through 1995.

Sarkozy returned to government in 2002, when he became interior minister and then finance minister in 2004 under President Jacques Chirac. In 2007, Sarkozy ran for and won the presidency, succeeding Chirac.

Sarkozy is known almost as well for his personal life as for his political career. He has been married three times, most recently to singer Carla Bruni.

MAJOR POLITICAL PARTIES AND CURRENT LEADERS

The individuals charged with enforcing the constitution and operating the government must be elected by French voters. Free and fair elections

are held, and there are few restrictions on how political parties can be organized and run.

Like many other countries, France has a free, active, multiparty system. The main political parties are the Socialist Party, the Union for a Popular Movement, and the Union for French Democracy. Some of the issues that separate one political party from another are the size and role of the government, the state of the economy, the country's place on the world stage, the nation's defense, the quality of the environment, and the protection of personal freedoms.

In the election that took place in April 2007, 12 candidates competed to replace President Jacques Chirac. In May, the two highest vote-getters—Nicolas Sarkozy and Ségolène Royal—faced each other in a runoff election. Despite the fact that many of the candidates who lost the preliminary round threw their support behind Royal, Sarkozy won, with more than 53 percent of the vote. Upon taking office, President Sarkozy appointed François Fillon to the position of prime minister.

The French Socialist Party conducts a campaign rally before the 2010 regional elections in Paris.

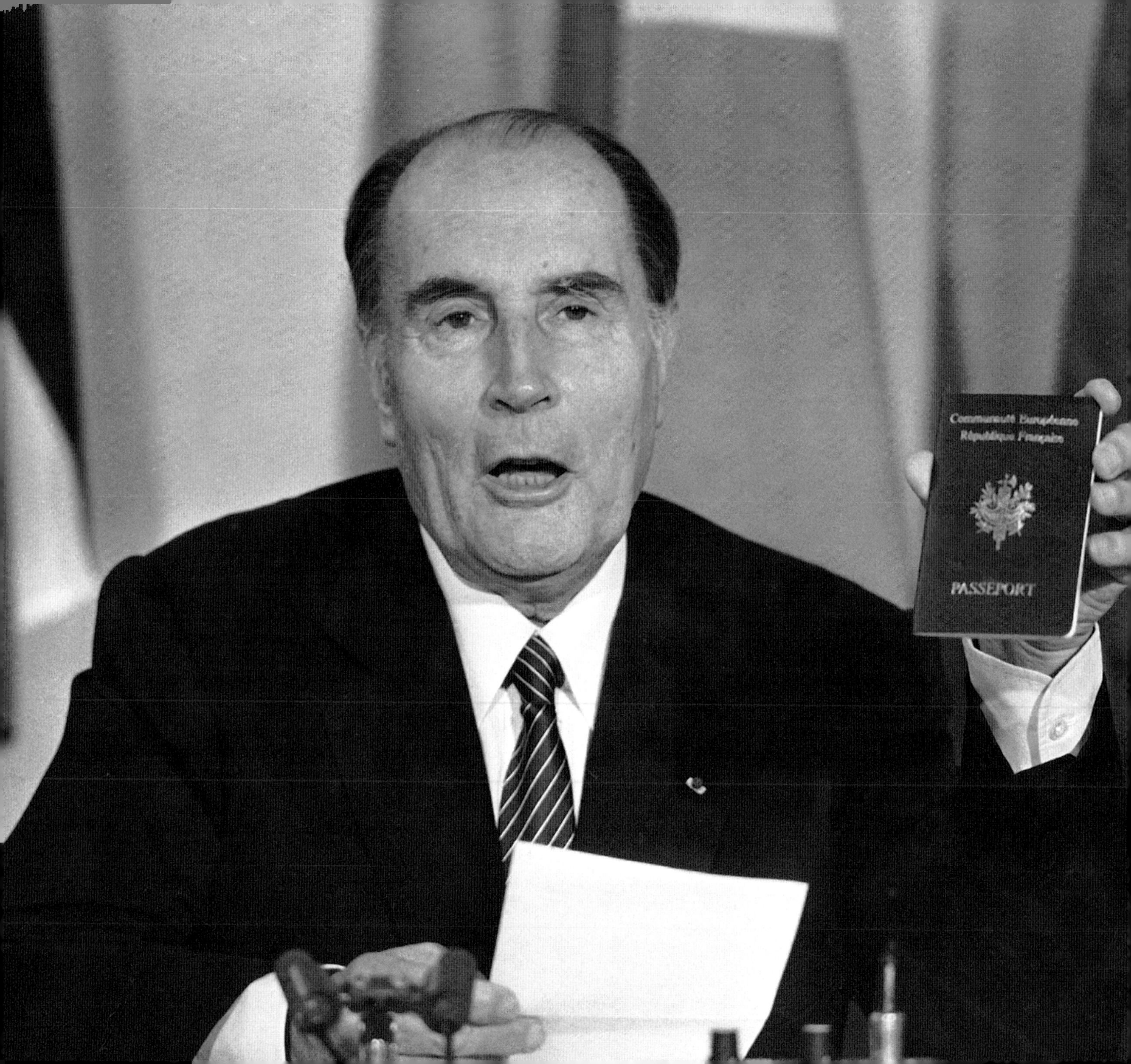
PASSEPORT

CHAPTER 8

ECONOMICS: IN SOCIALISM'S SHADOW

Historically, France has been recognized as one of the most socialized economies in the West. Socialism took hold when François Mitterrand of the Socialist Party was elected president and enacted a program of nationalization. With the goal of economic growth, the French government took over 12 industrial conglomerates and several dozen banks. The state came to own or partially own a long list of companies, including two airlines, an automobile manufacturer, and various utilities. In 2010, France had the world's fifth-largest economy, with a gross domestic product (GDP) of $2.66 trillion.[1]

Many of these businesses have been privatized again, as the government has stepped back from business ownership and taken steps toward a more capitalist approach. While the French government is still involved in the power, public transportation, and defense industries, it

President François Mitterrand, pictured in 1984, was a major force behind socializing the French economy.

ECONOMIC FREEDOM

In 2010, France ranked sixty-fourth of 179 countries in the Heritage Foundation's Index of Economic Freedom.[2] The index measures how much control citizens of a country have over their employment and property. According to the Heritage Foundation, the French government still plays a major role in the economy, accounting for more than half of national spending. The government is a significant shareholder in some industries. However, France's economic freedom ranking has improved slightly since President Nicolas Sarkozy started enacting reforms to privatize some portions of the economy.

has mostly left the banking and insurance sectors. The government still maintains partial ownership of major transportation and telecommunication companies, but it has reduced its financial investment in them.

The French government has continued to be involved in the economy in other ways, however. To bolster economic growth and to combat unemployment, the parliament passed a $35 billion stimulus plan in February 2009. The plan centered on investment in infrastructure and tax breaks for small businesses. The government also established a $25 billion investment fund to protect vulnerable French companies from foreign takeovers. The president has also proposed another fund to provide $52 billion for investment in the science and technology fields. Although these plans may benefit business and the economy in the short term, some economists fear that the heightened level of state involvement and spending will lead to worse financial difficulties in the future.

In 1998, France implemented a 35-hour workweek, and hours worked beyond that were to be paid as overtime. In addition to freeing up more time for leisure, the law was intended to combat unemployment by requiring more workers to be hired. However, conservative opponents of the law argued that it was damaging to businesses and hampered economic growth. The payment of state subsidies helped offset business owners' costs but at taxpayers' expense. The government changed approaches in October 2007, when it encouraged French workers to put in longer hours by lowering the payroll taxes for those who worked more than 35 hours. In 2008, employers gained more flexibility in enforcing overtime on their employees. Proponents of a longer workweek hoped to boost the economy, reasoning that French workers would put in more hours, bring home more pay, and thus spend more money.

FRANCE AND THE EUROPEAN UNION

In 1950, after reflecting on France's devastation in World Wars I and II, the nation's foreign minister, Robert Schuman, proposed creation of an organization meant to prevent another war with Germany. That organization, called the European Coal and Steel Community, was formed when representatives from France, West Germany, Italy, Belgium, Luxembourg, and the Netherlands signed the Treaty of Paris in 1951. As Europe's first supranational community, the organization created a common market for the sale of coal and steel.

France began using euros as its official currency in 2002.

In 1967, the European Coal and Steel Community became part of the European Economic Community. Fifteen years later, in 1992, with the strong encouragement of President François Mitterrand, French voters approved the Maastricht Treaty, which intended to bring together the European Coal and Steel Community and the European Economic Community to form the European Union (EU). The next year, the treaty was approved by the required number of countries, and the EU was born.

France was one of the EU's founding members. On January 1, 2002, France replaced its franc with the euro, the currency issued by the EU. In 2008, Sarkozy served a six-month term as the EU's president. As a member of the EU, France has a ready market for its goods and services, as well as a source for obtaining the items it cannot produce in the quantities it needs.

NATURAL RESOURCES AND INDUSTRIES

France has some of the most productive farmland in western Europe, and much of the country is agricultural. France is the world's second-largest producer of agricultural products, after the United States.[3] Grain farms are prevalent in northern France, and dairy, pork, poultry, and apple products come from the western region. Corn, fruits, vegetables, and wine make up a large portion of agricultural products from the south of France. Central France is known for its beef production.

Tourism is France's largest industry. More than 75 million people visit the country each year, more than any other country.[4] Tourists

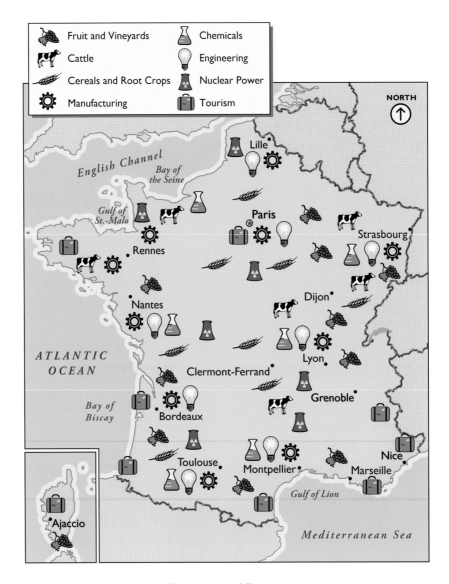

Legend:

- 🍇 Fruit and Vineyards
- 🐄 Cattle
- 🌾 Cereals and Root Crops
- ⚙️ Manufacturing
- ⚗️ Chemicals
- 💡 Engineering
- ☢️ Nuclear Power
- 🧳 Tourism

NORTH ↑

English Channel

Bay of the Seine

Gulf of St.-Malo

Lille

Paris

Strasbourg

Rennes

Nantes

Dijon

ATLANTIC OCEAN

Clermont-Ferrand

Lyon

Bay of Biscay

Bordeaux

Grenoble

Toulouse

Montpellier

Nice

Marseille

Gulf of Lion

Ajaccio

Mediterranean Sea

Resources of France

are drawn by special events, such as Paris fashion shows, the Cannes international film festival, and the Tour de France cycling competition. Paris is the world's most visited city.

France's other major industries involve the production of machinery, chemicals, automobiles, metallurgy, aircraft, electronics, textiles, and foods. France's natural resources include coal, iron ore, bauxite, zinc, uranium, antimony, arsenic, potash, feldspar, flurospar, and gypsium. Timber and fish are also plentiful.

INFRASTRUCTURE

France takes pride in its highly developed infrastructure, including communication and transportation systems, and the government has a history of investing in these systems. In 2009, the government continued this practice by investing in projects designed to support transportation.

Both visitors to and residents of France benefit from a well-developed transportation system. The country has 638,262 miles (1,027,183 km) of paved roadways and 18,152 miles (29,213 km) of railways.[5] In addition, there are 474 airports in France—297 with paved runways and 177 without.[6] The country has 5,282 miles (8,501 km) of waterways, and most of the harbors can handle ships large enough to carry freight.[7]

France also has a well-developed communication system. In 2009, 35,500,000 landline telephones were in use, along with 59,543,000 cell phones.[8] An estimated 44,625,000 French people were Internet users.[9]

Utilities such as gas, electricity, and water are efficiently delivered to consumers. Most of France's electricity is produced through nuclear power.

THE TOUR DE FRANCE

The Tour de France, first held in 1903, is an annual bicycle race held in France and nearby countries. Teams of cyclists ride approximately 2,156 miles (3,471 km) during the three-week race. The racecourse changes each year but always ends in Paris.

The Tour de France is divided into stages, and each stage lasts one day. Each rider's time is clocked each day, and his cumulative total is tallied across the race. Each day, the rider with the lowest cumulative time is recognized by being allowed to wear the yellow jersey for that stage of the race. Monetary prizes are awarded to the winners of the stages and to the overall winner of the race.

IMPORTS AND EXPORTS

France is the second-largest trading nation in western Europe (after Germany) and fifth largest in the world. In 2009, it imported an estimated $535.8 billion in goods, and exports were valued at $473.9 billion.[10]

France's primary imports are machinery and other equipment, as well as vehicles, crude oil, aircraft, plastics, and chemicals. Most imports come from other members of the EU. In 2009,

France's biggest import partners were EU members Germany (19.41 percent), Belgium (11.61 percent), Italy (7.97 percent), the Netherlands (7.15 percent), Spain (6.68 percent), and the United Kingdom (4.9 percent).[11] Other imports came from the United States (4.72 percent) and China (4.4 percent).[12]

France's main exports are machinery and transportation equipment, aircraft, plastics, chemicals, pharmaceutical products, beverages, and iron and steel. In 2009, the major purchasers of these products were Germany (15.88 percent), Italy (8.16 percent), Spain (7.8 percent), Belgium (7.44 percent), the United Kingdom (7.04 percent), and the United States (5.65 percent).[13]

INCOME AND POVERTY

In 2009, the per capita income in France was $32,500, a slight decrease from 2007 and 2008. The country's unemployment rate increased from 7.4 percent in 2008 to 9.5 percent in 2010. In 2004, a reported 6.2 percent lived below the poverty line.[14]

According to the National Institute of Statistics and Economic Studies, the poverty line in France is set at half the median income. Historically, those living beneath the poverty line have included the elderly, owners of small businesses, and farmers. Social programs have helped many of these individuals. In addition, the French government has provided benefits guaranteeing individuals a minimum income. Having this

A nuclear power plant in Montélimar, France

support has ended the poverty cycle for some families, including those of unskilled workers and single parents.

In recent years, the face of poverty in France has changed. Although the long-term unemployed and those with a family history of receiving public assistance are still among France's poorest residents, many of today's poor are immigrants. People from northern Africa and sub-Saharan Africa come to France with few of the skills needed to get jobs. Similarly, many people from Romania and elsewhere, who enter France under the Schengen Agreement, often do not have marketable skills. Some of the extremely poor live in bidonvilles, shantytowns on the outskirts of French towns. In 2010, President Sarkozy began a controversial program to relocate residents of bidonvilles back to their home countries.

Two Frenchmen invented the hot air balloon in 1783.

CHALLENGES

France's economic challenges are similar to those faced by other developed countries. Increasing unemployment, a rising trade deficit, and growing the domestic economy are among the key issues faced by the French government. Some of these issues have resulted from the country's history of a relatively open immigration policy and generous social programs. The current government has been tackling these challenges with stimulus programs and investment. However, most economists and other financial experts do not believe these measures

CHAMPAGNE

Beverages are a major export of France, and champagne is one of them. France wants to keep its hold on this market—and its reputation as the home of fine champagne—by making sure the word *champagne* is used only for sparkling wines from the Champagne region that are made according to Comité Interprofessionel du Vin de Champagne regulations. In the EU and many other countries, the name *champagne* is legally protected by the 1891 Treaty of Madrid. The right to use this name was reaffirmed in the Treaty of Versailles, which was agreed to shortly after World War I, and many countries follow this practice. In the United States, using the word *champagne* to label other products is illegal, unless the producer had permission to do so before 2006. Each label must include the location where the wine was made, however.

will provide long-term solutions to the country's financial problems.

Yet another challenge is the decrease in exports brought on by France's lack of competitiveness on the international stage. While other countries have experienced a decrease in exports because of a loss of market share, France's problem has been caused primarily by two other factors: the nation's slowness to respond to an increase in foreign demand and its policy of encouraging production work to move offshore.

It will not be easy for France to regain its competitive edge and thereby increase its export potential. According to some economists, the country must encourage research, development, and innovation; reduce the tax burden; and create conditions that will spur rapid business growth.

Demonstrators protest the French government's policies on unemployment and job security in May 2010.

CHAPTER 9
FRANCE TODAY

In the United States, many people live for their work. In France, leisure time is as important as work life, if not more important. Food is to be enjoyed as a complete dining experience, not a rushed affair. And although religion is important in France, it does not have the emphasis it has in parts of the United States. These are among the things American visitors to France may have trouble getting used to, especially if planning an extended stay or a move.

Despite the French fondness for having fun, doing work is necessary. Yet despite recent efforts to lengthen the workweek in France, most employees work fewer than 40 hours. And instead of having two or three weeks of vacation a year, most French workers have five. Until recently, most workers in France retired at age 60. In the fall of 2010, a law was passed to raise the retirement age to 62, leading to weeks of demonstrations and strikes. In the United States, by comparison, the age to receive full retirement benefits is 67.

The French people are known for placing a priority on leisure time.

French students protest raising the retirement age from 60 to 62 in 2010.

The workday is also more generous in France. In some areas of the country, workers take long lunches. Many times, people go home for lunch or eat at a nearby restaurant or café. While the French enjoy their more leisurely lifestyle, some critics have argued that these practices have held France back in terms of economic advancement and productivity.

When not working, the French take advantage of the many cultural resources available to them. Movies, dance clubs, and theaters are all popular. Many French love to travel, as well, whether to domestic or international destinations.

EDUCATION

Education in France is a high priority. In 2009, approximately 99 percent of the French population over age 15 could read and write.[1] Attending school is required for children between ages 6 and 16, but many students start school younger and continue on to higher education.

Schools in France can be very competitive, and

HIGHER EDUCATION

French students have several options for higher education following lycée. France has 91 public universities and 175 professional schools.[2] Students who complete university training are awarded a *licence*, which is equivalent to a bachelor's degree from a US college. Students who continue their studies beyond that can work toward a *maîtrise* (master's degree) or a doctorate.

children get an early start. Many children begin their education at age two, although doing so is not required. *École maternelles* are similar to a kindergarten or preschool. They get children between ages two and six ready for primary school. These children study reading and writing and learn their numbers. They also spend time on art and other creative projects.

Between ages six and 11, children attend the *école primaire*, or primary school. These children study the same subjects as children in other countries, but they also study a foreign language—usually, English. In the past, students attended school Monday and Tuesday, had Wednesdays off, and then went back to school Thursday through Saturday morning. But in September 2008, Saturday classes were ended, and primary schools moved to a four-day schedule. Students at this level spend approximately 28 hours per week in class.

Between ages 11 and 15, students attend *collège*, or middle school. Collège provides students with a basic secondary education, and classes include math, language, history, and science. In collège, students can decide if they want to continue in a school that is more academically focused and prepare for a professional career or go to one that is more technically focused and prepare for a trade- or service-oriented career. When students have finished their collège classes, they take a final exam. After that, they decide whether to continue their education or, if they are at least 16 years old, to leave school.

The official motto of France is "Liberty, Equality, Fraternity."

A mother walks her two young children to school in Paris.

HOURS IN SCHOOL

Most French students attend school between the hours of 8:30 a.m. and 4:30 p.m. Some schools, however, hold classes until 5:00 or 6:00 p.m., depending on the age of the students and the course of study.

Students do not have to worry about getting out of school in time to participate in extracurricular activities, because most schools in France do not have them. Being involved in sports, music, and other activities is not viewed as important to students' education.

The lycée is equivalent to a high school in the United States. There are three types of lycée. The *lycée général* prepares students for further formal education, usually at a university. The coursework is a continuation of that offered in collège, with the addition of philosophy; all students are required to demonstrate an understanding of philosophy before graduation. In the *lycée technique,* a narrowly focused technical path is added to the traditional criteria. The *lycée professionnel* provides a vocational option for students who are thinking about getting a job after graduation, rather than more education.

After a sometimes stressful day at a competitive school, teens are more than ready to enjoy themselves. During their nonschool hours, they listen to music, go bicycling, swim, and visit museums and other cultural resources. Teens from families in lower income brackets may also be expected to work to supplement the family's income, and those who live on small farms will likely be responsible for doing some chores.

A young French woman relaxes on a bench at the Champs-Élysées Park in Paris.

UNEMPLOYMENT AND VIOLENCE

One of the side effects of increasing unemployment in France has been violence. In July 2010, hundreds of police responded to two nights of rioting in Grenoble, a historic city at the foot of the Alps. Many experts fear that as long as unemployment remains high and job prospects remain low, violence will continue. Others believe that the problem is an ethnic one and that unemployment is not the key issue. They reason, for example, that if Algerian immigrants drop out of school and remain unskilled, providing more job opportunities will not help them find work.

CHALLENGES FOR THE COUNTRY

France is a beautiful and exciting country, with many things to see and do. France also has a long and storied history. It is the birthplace of many cultural movements and has helped develop and support many others. But despite its sophisticated image, France has some problems, too.

France must reduce its high level of deficit spending, which threatens its economy. France must also address the rising costs of its many social programs, which have historically been provided to aid citizens in need. The nation can no longer afford to offer aid at the same levels as in the past.

France's leaders have put in place economic policies intended to reduce unemployment and poverty, two of the country's major problems. Both problems have been blamed for increasing violence, sometimes deadly, in the bidonvilles around France's major cities and suburbs. The French government has also taken steps to deal with the nation's large and growing immigrant population. Many of France's unemployed people are immigrants, especially Muslims. The violence associated with unemployment and poverty has stirred anti-Muslim feelings in France, even when there is no Muslim connection.

France has a history of lenient and open immigration, but the government is now rethinking that policy. The government has also implemented a controversial policy regarding the nation's Muslim population. The French constitution clearly states that the country is and shall remain secular. Given this, many French consider it a violation of the law to wear religious symbols in public places. The government has passed laws that prohibit wearing items that can be

A Muslim woman walks in Avignon, France, wearing a full-face veil.

A rainbow is seen through the clouds over the Place de la Concorde square in Paris.

considered religious. But instead of easing racial and ethnic tensions, these laws may end up having the opposite effect.

Despite these challenges, the future of France seems positive. Even in a period of almost worldwide economic downturn, tourists still flock to France and tourism dollars help boost the nation's economy. The French government has recognized the country's challenges and made efforts to deal with them. The measures have not always proved popular among France's leaders or citizens, but most realize that something must be done to ensure the nation's economic future.

CARRYING SECULARISM TOO FAR?

In October 2010, the French Constitutional Council upheld a law that banned wearing a burka, a face-covering veil worn by some Muslim women. A woman found wearing a burka could be fined 150 euros (US$190) or required to complete a citizenship course. If someone else forced the woman to wear it, such as her husband or father, he could be fined up to 15,000 euros (US$19,000).

In 2004, the French government passed a law that banned the wearing or displaying of overtly religious symbols in schools. Among the items girls can no longer wear are head scarves. According to the government, this law was necessary because the constitution requires the country to be secular.

Not everyone agrees with the law, however. Some see the law as an example of discrimination against France's growing Muslim population. And others think that people who insist that women wear a burka are in fact attacking France's policy of secularism.

TIMELINE

4500 BCE	Neolithic villages are built along the west coast of what is now France.
51 BCE	Julius Caesar and his forces put Gaul under Roman control.
486 CE	King Clovis defeats the Romans and establishes the Merovingian dynasty.
800	On December 25, Pope Leo III crowns Charlemagne emperor of the Western Roman Empire.
1337	The Hundred Years' War begins.
1763	The Seven Years' War ends with the Treaty of Paris.
1789	On July 14, French citizens storm the Bastille prison, beginning the French Revolution.
1793	On August 10, the Louvre opens officially as a museum.
1848	The Gallic rooster, a symbol of France, appears on the country's seal.
1889	On March 31, the Eiffel Tower is unveiled.
1903	On May 31, the first Tour de France begins; it is completed on July 5.
1914	On August 3, Germany declares war on France, and France enters World War I.

1918	On November 11, an armistice is signed, ending conflict with Germany.
1944	On June 6, Allies land on Normandy Beach in the D-day invasion.
1944	On August 25, Paris is liberated from Nazi control.
1951	On April 18, the Treaty of Paris is signed, establishing the European Coal and Steel Community.
1958	On May 13, the Fourth Republic collapses.
1958	On October 4, the French constitution of the Fifth Republic is adopted.
1958	On December 21, Charles de Gaulle is elected president of France.
1981	President François Mitterrand takes office and begins nationalizing French industries.
1993	The European Union is formed, with France as a founding member.
1998	On April 29, France signs the Kyoto Protocol.
2002	On January 1, the euro becomes the common currency of France.
2007	On May 7, Nicolas Sarkozy is elected president.

FACTS AT YOUR FINGERTIPS

GEOGRAPHY

Official name: French Republic (in French, République Française)

Size: 248,429 square miles (643,427 sq km)

Climate: Generally cool winters and mild summers, but mild winters and hot summers along the Mediterranean; occasional strong, cold wind known as the mistral

Highest elevation: Mont Blanc, 15,771 feet (4,807 m) above sea level

Lowest elevation: Rhône River delta, 6.5 feet (-2 m) below sea level

Significant geographic features: Pyrenees, Alps

PEOPLE

Population (July 2011 est.): 64,768,389

Most populous city: Paris

Ethnic groups: Celtic and Latin with Teutonic, Slavic, North African, Indochinese, and Basque minorities

Percentage of residents living in urban areas: 77 percent

Life expectancy: 81.09 years (world rank: 12)

Language: French

Religions: Roman Catholic, 83–88 percent; Protestant, 2 percent; Muslim, 5–10 percent; Jewish, 1 percent; unaffiliated, 4 percent

GOVERNMENT AND ECONOMY

Government: republic

Date of adoption of current constitution: September 28, 1958

Capital: Paris

Head of state: president

Head of government: prime minister

Legislature: Parliament, consists of the Senate and the National Assembly

Currency: euro

Industries and natural resources: agriculture, machinery, chemicals, automobiles, metallurgy, aircraft, electronics, textiles, food processing, tourism, nuclear energy

NATIONAL SYMBOLS

Holidays: Bastille Day (July 14) celebrates the 1789 storming of the Bastille during the French Revolution. World War II Victory Day is celebrated on May 8, while World War I Armistice Day is November 11.

Flag: three vertical stripes of blue, white, and red

National anthem: "La Marseillaise"

National symbol: Gallic rooster

KEY PEOPLE

Joan of Arc (circa 1412–1431), rallied French troops against the British during the Hundred Years' War

Napoléon I (1769–1821), expanded the French empire through the Napoleonic Wars

Charles de Gaulle (1890–1970), established the Fifth Republic

RÉGION; CAPITAL

Alsace; Strasbourg

Aquitaine; Bordeaux

Auvergne; Clermont-Ferrand

Basse-Normandie; Caen

Burgundy; Dijon

Brittany; Rennes

Centre; Orléans

Champagne-Ardenne; Châlons-en-Champagne

Corsica; Ajaccio

Franche-Comté; Besançon

Guadeloupe; Basse-Terre

French Guiana; Cayenne

Haute-Normandie; Rouen

Île-de-France; Paris

Languedoc-Roussillon; Montpellier

Limousin; Limoges

Lorraine; Metz

Martinique; Fort-de-France

Midi-Pyrénées; Toulouse

Nord-Pas-de-Calais; Lille

Pays de la Loire; Nantes

Picardy; Amiens

Poitou-Charentes; Poitiers

Provence-Alpes-Côte d'Azur; Marseille

Réunion; Saint-Denis

Rhône-Alpes; Lyon

GLOSSARY

armistice

A temporary suspension of hostility by agreement between opponents.

divine right

The idea that a monarch receives the right to rule directly from God and not from the people.

estuary

A water passage where a river meets a body of water.

feudalism

A system of political organization in which a lord's subjects received protection in exchange for their service during war.

indigenous

Originally or naturally belonging to an area.

Neolithic

Relating to the latest period of the Stone Age.

nobility

A class of people of high birth or rank.

Paleolithic

Relating to the earliest period of the Stone Age.

plateau

A hill or mountain with a flat top.

preamble

An introductory statement of a constitution or law that explains its intent.

privateer

An armed private ship authorized to attack enemy shipping, or a sailor on such a ship.

protectorate

A country or region that is defended and controlled by a more powerful country or region.

referendum

A vote by an entire electorate on a specific question or questions.

reparation

Compensation for a wrong.

revolution

The overthrow of one government for another government that differs in ideologies.

secular

Nonreligious.

socialism

An economic system in which the government controls the means of production and distribution of goods.

topography

The physical and natural features of an area.

urbanization

The process of becoming more citylike.

ADDITIONAL RESOURCES

SELECTED BIBLIOGRAPHY

Brown, Frederick. *For the Soul of France: Cultural Wars in the Age of Dreyfus*. New York: Knopf, 2010. Print.

Carlyle, Thomas. *The French Revolution: A History*. London: Modern Library, 1837. Print.

Doyle, William. *The Oxford History of the French Revolution*. New York: Oxford UP, 1989. Print.

Robb, Graham. *The Discovery of France: A Historical Geography from the Revolution to the First World War*. New York: Norton, 2007. Print.

"The World Factbook: France." *Central Intelligence Agency*. Central Intelligence Agency, 29 Dec. 2010. Web.

FURTHER READINGS

Corona, Laurel. *France*. Farmington Hills, MI: Lucent, 2004. Print.

Egendorf, Laura K., ed. *The French Revolution: Opposing Viewpoints in World History*. Farmington Hills, MI: Greenhaven, 2003. Print.

Roberts, William J. *France: A Reference Guide from the Renaissance to the Present*. New York: Facts on File, 2004. Print.

WEB LINKS

To learn more about France, visit ABDO Publishing Company online at **www.abdopublishing.com**. Web sites about France are featured on our Book Links page. These links are routinely monitored and updated to provide the most current information available.

PLACES TO VISIT

If you are ever in France, consider checking out these important and interesting sites!

Eiffel Tower

Designed as the entrance to the Universal Exposition of 1889, the Eiffel Tower is a communication tower that provides one of the best views of Paris.

Louvre Museum

The Louvre is one of the most famous art museums in the world and includes works such as the *Mona Lisa*.

Normandy American Cemetery and Memorial

The cemetery and memorial, which stand on a cliff overlooking Omaha Beach, honor servicemen who lost their lives storming the coast of Normandy on D-day.

[SOURCE NOTES]

CHAPTER 1. A VISIT TO FRANCE

1. "Paris." *Encyclopædia Britannica*. Encyclopædia Britannica, 2011. Web. 9 Mar. 2011.

CHAPTER 2. GEOGRAPHY: JEWEL OF WESTERN EUROPE

1. "The World Factbook: France." *Central Intelligence Agency*. Central Intelligence Agency, 29 Dec. 2010. Web. 8 Feb. 2011.

2. "Country Guide: France." *BBC: Weather*. BBC, n.d. Web. 8 Feb. 2011.

3. Ibid.

4. "The World Factbook: France." *Central Intelligence Agency*. Central Intelligence Agency, 29 Dec. 2010. Web. 8 Feb. 2011.

5. "Champagne-Ardenne." *Encyclopædia Britannica*. Encyclopædia Britannica, 2011. Web. 9 Mar. 2011.

6. "Loire River." *Encyclopædia Britannica*. Encyclopædia Britannica, 2011. Web. 9 Mar. 2011.

7. "The River Loire." *Burgundytoday.com*. Burgundy Today, n.d. Web. 5 Feb. 2011.

8. "Seine River." *Encyclopædia Britannica*. Encyclopædia Britannica, 2011. Web. 9 Mar. 2011.

9. "Country Guide: France." *BBC: Weather*. BBC, n.d. Web. 8 Feb. 2011.

10. "Garonne River." *Encyclopædia Britannica*. Encyclopædia Britannica, 2011. Web. 9 Mar. 2011.

11. "The World Factbook: France." *Central Intelligence Agency*. Central Intelligence Agency, 29 Dec. 2010. Web. 8 Feb. 2011.

12. "Garonne River." *Encyclopædia Britannica*. Encyclopædia Britannica, 2011. Web. 9 Mar. 2011.

13. "Population by District from 1990 to 2011." *City Council of Paris*. City Council of Paris, 1 Jan. 2011. Web. 9 Mar. 2011.

14. "Marseille." *Encyclopædia Britannica*. Encyclopædia Britannica, 2011. Web. 9 Mar. 2011.

15. "Lyon." *Encyclopædia Britannica*. Encyclopædia Britannica, 2011. Web. 9 Mar. 2011.

16. "Toulouse." *Encyclopædia Britannica*. Encyclopædia Britannica, 2011. Web. 9 Mar. 2011.

CHAPTER 3. ANIMALS AND NATURE: PRESERVING ECOSYSTEMS

1. "The Gallic Rooster." *Government Portal.* Service d'Information du Gouvernement, France, 4 June 2007. Web. 29 December 2011.

2. "Summary Statistics: Summaries by Country, Table 5, Threatened Species in Each Country." *IUCN Red List of Threatened Species.* International Union for Conservation of Nature and Natural Resources, 2010. Web. 8 Feb. 2011.

3. "National Parks of France." *Parcs Nationaux de France.* Parcs Nationaux de France, n.d. Web. 9 Mar. 2011.

CHAPTER 4. HISTORY: KINGS, CONQUERORS, AND REVOLUTIONARIES

None

CHAPTER 5. PEOPLE: THE CHANGING FACE OF THE FRENCH

1. "The World Factbook: France." *Central Intelligence Agency.* Central Intelligence Agency, 29 Dec. 2010. Web. 8 Feb. 2011.

2. "Annual Census Surveys 2004 and 2005." *Institut National de la Statistique et des études Economiques.* Institut National de la Statistique et des études Economiques, Aug. 2006. Web. 1 Jan. 2011.

3. "The World Factbook: France." *Central Intelligence Agency.* Central Intelligence Agency, 29 Dec. 2010. Web. 8 Feb. 2011.

4. Ibid.

5. Ibid.

6. Ibid.

7. Ibid.

CHAPTER 6. CULTURE: WHERE HISTORIC MEETS CHIC

1. "French Cuisine Quotes." *FoodReference.com*. FoodReference.com, n.d. Web. 4 Jan. 2011.

CHAPTER 7. POLITICS: THE FIFTH REPUBLIC

1. "Constitution of October 4, 1958." *Assemblée Nationale*. Assemblée Nationale, n.d. Web. 4 Jan. 2011.

CHAPTER 8. ECONOMICS: IN SOCIALISM'S SHADOW

1. "Background Note: France." *US Department of State*. US Department of State, 18 Aug. 2010. Web. 8 Feb. 2011.

2. Index of Economic Freedom Rankings. *2011 Index of Economic Freedom*. Heritage Foundation, 2011. Web. 6 Feb. 2011.

3. "Background Note: France." *US Department of State*. US Department of State, 18 Aug. 2010. Web. 8 Feb. 2011.

4. "The World Factbook: France." *Central Intelligence Agency*. Central Intelligence Agency, 29 Dec. 2010. Web. 8 Feb. 2011.

5. Ibid.

6. Ibid.

7. Ibid.

8. Ibid.

9. Ibid.

10. Ibid.

11. Ibid.

12. Ibid.

13. Ibid.

14. Ibid.

CHAPTER 9. FRANCE TODAY

1. "The World Factbook: France." *Central Intelligence Agency.* Central Intelligence Agency, 29 Dec. 2010. Web. 8 Feb. 2011.

2. "Background Note: France." *US Department of State.* US Department of State, 18 Aug. 2010. Web. 8 Feb. 2011.

INDEX

PHOTO CREDITS